A Benjamin Blog and his Inquisitive Dog Guide

Russia

Anita Ganeri

heinemann
raintree

To contact Capstone Global Library please phone 800-747-4992, or visit our website
www.capstonepub.com

Edited by Helen Cox Cannons
Designed by Philippa Jenkins and Tim Bond
Original illustrations © Capstone Global Library Limited 2015
Original map illustration by Oxford Designers and Illustrators
Ben and Barko Illustrated by Sernur ISIK
Picture research by Svetlana Zhurkin
Production by Helen McCreath
Originated by Capstone Global Library Limited

Library of Congress Cataloging-in-Publication Data
Ganeri, Anita, 1961-
  Russia / Anita Ganeri.
    pages cm.—(Country guides, with Benjamin Blog and his inquisitive dog)
  Includes bibliographical references and index.
  ISBN 978-1-4109-7997-1 (hb)—ISBN 978-1-4109-8003-8 (pb)—ISBN 978-1-4109-8014-4 (ebook)
1. Russia (Federation)—Juvenile literature. I. Title.

DK510.23.G36 2015
947—dc23   2014043979

This book has been officially leveled by using the F&P Text Level Gradient™ Leveling System.

Acknowledgments
We would like to thank the following for permission to reproduce photographs: Alamy: Asia Photopress,
13, John Warburton-Lee Photography, 22; Dreamstime: Boris Akhunov, 15, Iakov Filimonov, 16; iStockphoto:
Lara111, 24; Newscom: Zuma Press/ITAR-TASS/Vladimir Smirnov, 23, Zuma Press/Russian Look/Konstantin
Mikhailov, 9; Shutterstock: Alex Alekseev, cover, Art Konovalov, 6, Dmitry Kosorukov, 18, Elena Shchipkova,
27, 29, Inna Felker, 14, Irina Afonskaya, 19, Jenoche, 17, MAR007, 21, mironov, 11, R3BV, 7, Serg Zastavkin, 10,
Tatiana Grozetskaya, 26, trubach, 28, Valeriya Popova, 4, 12, withGod, 8; Svetlana Zhurkin, 20, 25.

Every effort has been made to contact copyright holders of any material reproduced in this book. Any
omissions will be rectified in subsequent printings if notice is given to the publisher.

Some words are shown in bold, **like this.** You can find
out what they mean by looking in the glossary.

007332CTPSF15

Contents

Welcome to Russia!

Hello! My name is Benjamin Blog, and this is Barko Polo, my **inquisitive** dog. (He is named after the ancient explorer **Marco Polo**.) We have just returned from our latest adventure—exploring Russia. We put this book together from some of the blog posts we wrote along the way.

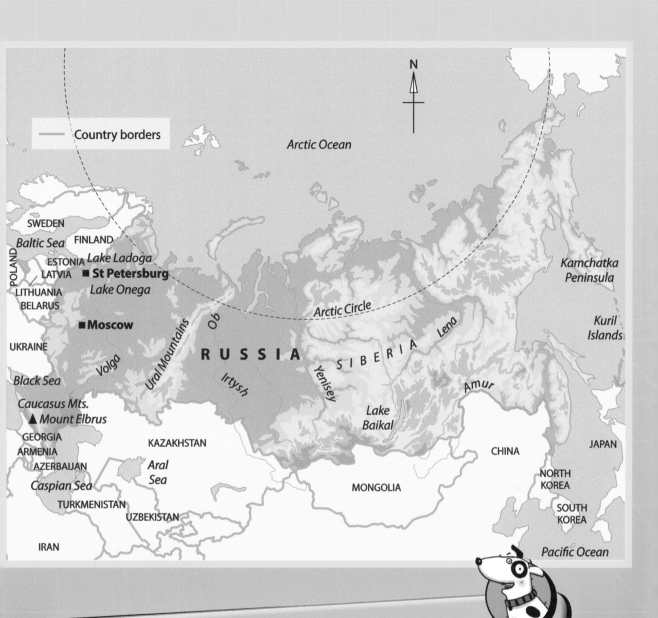

Country borders

Arctic Ocean

N

SWEDEN

Baltic Sea FINLAND

POLAND

ESTONIA *Lake Ladoga*
LATVIA ■ **St Petersburg**

LITHUANIA *Lake Onega*
BELARUS

■ **Moscow**

UKRAINE *Ural Mountains* *Ob* Arctic Circle

Lena

Volga **R U S S I A** S I B E R I A

Black Sea *Irtysh* *Yenisey* *Amur*

Caucasus Mts.
▲ *Mount Elbrus* *Lake Baikal*

GEORGIA
ARMENIA KAZAKHSTAN CHINA JAPAN
AZERBAIJAN *Aral Sea*

Caspian Sea NORTH KOREA

TURKMENISTAN MONGOLIA SOUTH KOREA
UZBEKISTAN

IRAN *Pacific Ocean*

Kamchatka Peninsula

Kuril Islands

BARKO'S BLOG-TASTIC RUSSIA FACTS

Russia is the world's largest country. It is so huge that it stretches across two **continents**—Europe and Asia. It has borders with 14 other countries, and coastlines with the Arctic Ocean and Pacific Ocean.

The Story of Russia

Posted by: Ben Blog | June 7 at 1:14 p.m.

Our tour began with a visit to St. Petersburg. What a beautiful city this is. This is the spectacular Peterhof Palace, which was built by Peter the Great. He ruled Russia as **tsar** then **emperor** from 1682 to 1725. During his reign, Russia became a huge and powerful empire.

BARKO'S BLOG-TASTIC RUSSIA FACTS

The Kremlin in Moscow is home to the Russian **president**. It is surrounded by high, red-brick walls and towers. Inside the Kremlin, there are four **gilt-domed** cathedrals and five grand palaces.

Lakes, Rivers, Forests, and Peaks

Posted by: Ben Blog | July 2 at 11:56 a.m.

From St. Petersburg, we made the long journey southeast to Lake Baikal. At 5,387 feet (1,642 meters), it is the world's deepest lake. It is also one of the oldest, at 25 million years old. The lake is home to some amazing animals. These seals are the only seals that live in fresh water.

BARKO'S BLOG-TASTIC RUSSIA FACTS

There are more than 100,000 rivers in Russia. The longest is the Lena River, which flows for 2,734 miles (4,399 kilometers). It starts in the Baikal Mountains and flows to the Laptev Sea, part of the Arctic Ocean.

Heading north, we reached the taiga, a huge, **coniferous** forest that covers much of Siberia. Even further north, the forest thins out and there are enormous plains, known as tundra. Here, it is so cold that the ground stays frozen for much of the year. Brrrr!

BARKO'S BLOG-TASTIC RUSSIA FACTS

The Ural Mountains are a mighty mountain range that runs for around 1,553 miles (2,500 kilometers), from the north to the south of Russia. The range forms a boundary between Europe and Asia.

City Tour

Posted by: Ben Blog | August 6 at 10:32 a.m.

Our next stop was Moscow, the capital city of Russia. It is famous for St. Basil's Cathedral, Red Square, the Kremlin, and lots more. The best way to get around is by Metro (underground train). We're here at Komsomolskaya Station—look at those **chandeliers**!

BARKO'S BLOG-TASTIC RUSSIA FACTS

Vladivostok, in the far southeast, is one of Russia's most important cities. It is Russia's biggest **port** on the Pacific Ocean and home to the Pacific Fleet (part of the Russian Navy).

Privet!

Most people in Russia speak Russian. *Privet!* (say "pree-VYET") means "Hi!" Russian is written in the Cyrillic alphabet. *Privet* is written like this: Привет! People in the different regions of Russia also speak their own local languages.

BARKO'S BLOG-TASTIC RUSSIA FACTS

More than 140 million people live in Russia. Most of them are Russians, but there are many other groups. These people are Tatars, wearing traditional dress. Tatars are Muslims and follow the religion of Islam.

In Russia, children start school when they are seven years old. Their first day at school is September 1, which is called Knowledge Day. It is marked by a special assembly. The children dress up and carry bunches of flowers for the teachers. A bell rings to welcome them to the school.

BARKO'S BLOG-TASTIC RUSSIA FACTS

Most Russian people live in cities, in large apartment buildings. Most apartments are quite small inside. In the countryside, many houses, churches, and schools are made from wood.

Many Russian people belong to the Russian Orthodox Church. Back in Moscow, we're paying a visit to the magnificent Cathedral of Christ the Savior. The cathedral was destroyed in 1931, but it was rebuilt in the 1990s. Thousands of people come here to worship.

BARKO'S BLOG-TASTIC RUSSIA FACTS

In February or March, Russians celebrate *Maslenitsa* (Pancake Week). There are snowball fights, sleigh rides, singing, dancing, and plenty of pancakes to eat.

Time for Lunch...

All that sightseeing made us hungry, so we decided to stop for lunch. Russia is famous for its soup. I ordered a bowl of *borscht*, which is made from beets. You can eat it hot or cold, with a dollop of sour cream, a sprig of **dill**, and a hunk of crusty rye bread.

BARKO'S BLOG-TASTIC RUSSIA FACTS

Blinis are thin pancakes topped with butter, sour cream, jam, or even caviar (fish eggs). The best caviar comes from fish called sturgeon, which live in the Caspian Sea, off western Russia.

Having Fun

Posted by: Ben Blog | December 29 at 7:45 p.m.

Our next stop was St. Petersburg. We have tickets for the ballet at the Mariinsky Theater. Russian ballet is famous around the world. We have come to watch the Mariinsky Ballet perform *Swan Lake.* This ballet tells the story of a princess who is turned into a swan.

BARKO'S BLOG-TASTIC RUSSIA FACTS

Sports are very popular in Russia. In 2014, the Winter Olympics were held in Sochi, in the south of Russia. The Russian team won the most medals— 13 gold, 11 silver, and 9 bronze.

From Drilling to Dolls

Posted by: Ben Blog | April 30 at 10:25 a.m.

We're taking the famous Trans-Siberia railroad through Siberia. This is where most of Russia's oil, coal, metals, diamonds, and gold come from. The train transports huge loads of minerals from Siberia to western Russia. It is the longest railroad line in the world.

BARKO'S BLOG-TASTIC RUSSIA FACTS

These Russian dolls are made from wood and get smaller and smaller. They are placed inside each other, in order of size. In Russian, they are called *matryoshkas*.

And Finally...

It is the last day of our trip, and we have traveled even further east to the Kamchatka Peninsula. I wanted to see the Valley of the **Geysers**, where many geysers gush up from the ground. The only way to reach the valley is by helicopter. Come on, Barko!

BARKO'S BLOG-TASTIC RUSSIA FACTS

St. Basil's Cathedral in Red Square, Moscow, is the most famous building in Russia. It was built between 1555 and 1561 and has brightly painted, onion-shaped **domes**. Amazing!

Russia Fact File

Area: 6,601,652 square miles
(17,098,200 square kilometers)

Population: 143,700,000 (2014)

Capital city: Moscow

Other main cities: St. Petersburg, Novosibirsk, Vladivostok, Yekaterinburg

Language: Russian

Main religion: Christianity (Russian Orthodox)

Highest mountain: Mount Elbrus
(18,510 feet/5,642 meters)

Longest river: Lena (2,648 miles/4,261 kilometers)

Currency: Ruble

Russia Quiz

Find out how much you know about Russia with our quick quiz.

1. How many countries have borders with Russia?
a) 4
b) 14
c) 24

2. Which is the deepest lake in the world?
a) Caspian Sea
b) Lake Superior
c) Lake Baikal

3. What does *Privet* mean?
a) Hi
b) Goodbye
c) How are you?

4. What is the main ingredient in *borscht*?
a) beets
b) cabbage
c) potatoes

5. What is this?

Glossary

chandelier large, grand light that hangs from the ceiling

coniferous type of tree with needles instead of leaves that stays green all year round

continent large area of land

dill leafy herb

dome rounded top of a tower on a building

emperor ruler of a group of countries, called an empire

geyser jet of hot water that shoots up from under the ground

gilt gold-like paint or material

inquisitive interested in learning about the world

Marco Polo explorer who lived from about 1254 to 1324. He traveled from Italy to China.

port place where ships are loaded and unloaded

president head of a country that is a republic

tsar name for the emperor of Russia before the year 1917

Find Out More

Books

Hunt, Jilly. *Russia* (Countries Around the World). Chicago: Heinemann Library, 2012.

Murray, Julie. *Russia* (Explore the Countries). Minneapolis: ABDO, 2014.

Ransome, Galya. *Russia in Our World* (Countries in Our World). Mankato, Minn.: Smart Apple Media, 2011.

Web sites

Facthound offers a safe, fun way to find Internet sites related to this book. All of the sites on Facthound have been researched by our staff.

Here's all you do:

Visit www.facthound.com

Type in this code: 9781410979971

Index